More praise for
"That'll Leave a Mark"

"Kevin Schumaker is a testament to "It gets greater later". His decision to become a poet at sixty years of age seems courageous but it was just inevitable. If you have heard him read his work at the various open mic events around town, you can't imagine him doing anything else.

That'll Leave a Mark is worth every second you spend with it. Please check out this poetry debut collection."
- *Yong Takahashi, Author of* **Observations Through Yellow Glasses**,
  founding editor of **Little Notes Lit Mag**
  @yongversation @littlenoteslitmag

"Kevin is the guy that will walk onto a $10,000 rug in a $1,000,000 house and pick up the corner to see all the dirt built up underneath. His resulting poem from the experience will focus on the beauty of the dirt and cast the house and the rug as the villain.

His perspective gives a new definition to beauty rarely found in today's society but deserves your attention."
- *Deanna Repose Oaks,*
  Author of **Don't Go; Stay**
  @deannareposeoaks

That'll Leave a Mark

That'll Leave a Mark

By Kevin Schumaker

for LaDonna - who puts up with my absurd dreams
and Ella - who dreams even bigger

Table of Contents

Introduction:

I have no interest in beauty
I don't know what to do with it
It is too much to be near

I prefer the face of the ugly
It is approachable and gentle
And it needs me as much as I need it

At an open mic event, a young Chinese woman read a poem about the mid-August Moon festival in her homeland. The poem was about the moon as a rabbit, sweet cakes, and falling in love. Her voice was soft and delicate, and her imagery summoned the feeling of an evening breeze across my cheek. Her gift humbled me.

She took the mic right after me, and while her poem was gentle and melodic, mine were much darker, with references to addiction, Lou Reed, Jack Kerouac, death, and failure. Her poem was a brightly colored finch singing in a tree, while mine were the bald black vultures that gather at the site of road kill and stare at you as you drive by slowly.

When she left the stage, I approached her to tell her how beautifully she writes. "Your poem was amazing," I stammered. "You capture beauty in a way I never can." She smiled graciously and replied, "Yours are beautiful, too; they are just about sadness."

I was stunned. I've never had a comment on my work that felt so perfectly complementary to what I try to do: capture the beauty in sadness, put into words what is elegant and gorgeous in the pain, frustration, disappointment, failure, and sorrow of life. If I can do this in any small way, I consider a poem a success.

It is evidence of my own psychological/emotional issues that I have never felt comfortable amongst the "perfect." Those people and things exhibit a classical reflection of success and accomplishment. The supermodel and the dashing leading man put me off. I am not comfortable amongst the well-mannered and well-spoken.

I grew up in a family that reached its social and economic peak by being able to buy a house just one block from the wealthy country club. My parents were so proud, only to have the house between us and the rolling manicured greens put up a ten-foot privacy fence, shutting us off from even a view of success.

And so, I grew up on the periphery of success. I was the poor (relatively) kid in the rich kids' school. I walked through their world of accomplishment to our home just outside the perimeter of their pride. Always an "almost made it. Always a "if only...." I was raised in a world where effort wasn't always enough. The treasures of the world are mana rained down on a select few. A special few, and they want nothing to do with us.

No, we were not the poorest. And yes, we had the advantages of a decent education and did not face the discrimination others had to endure. We were told we were welcome, only to have the door shut just as we arrived. Once, when I was denied a promotion at work, the man who made the choice said to me, almost in a hush and without meeting my eyes, "It was never going to be you." These are the words my parents and their parents before them might have heard. Or implicitly understood.

And so, I grew up to find beauty in other places. I learned to see it in the areas the special people ignore. I learned to conjure it from the bits and pieces the successful cast-off and reject. I learned to see it in the people that the special people reject—those like me, in the places I inhabit.

So, I prefer the mushrooms in my yard over the perfect lawn. I like the possum that invades the trash can at dusk and the beetle that shimmers when the sun hits it just right. I like the ugly, invasive, and disruptive.

Most of all, I love the broken and rejected people. I love the addict that is still using over the square that never has. I prefer the person who has stared into the abyss of depression over the one who gets out of bed easily. I'd rather spend time with the person whose true love left them over the couple that lives happily ever after.

I prefer the sadness.

I prefer the beauty of sadness.

Thus, the following collection of poems reflects this. They are about sadness and depression. I write of loves that were not to be and addictions too long indulged. I talk of sin and grace and the romance and disappointments of each. I write of life outside the perimeter of the beautiful world of moon festivals. I do so because there is a rabbit moon out here, too. He

is an alcoholic, taking it one day at a time, and he is
a treasure to know.

you write of a rabbit in the moon
and sweet cakes to share
and the nights you fall in love

I'm only comfortable with the discord
and the clash, and the loss
but all of my poems are about love as well

\-   Kevin, *February 2, 2025*

Marks

One Love

Simply strike one love
and all will be forgiven
I will not comment on it again

Simply strike one love
and imagine it has ended
and tell me I'm your only one

Simply strike one love
and damned be all the others
curled up in memories denied

Simply strike one love
and then please bring me flowers
forget-me-nots were never my style

Simply strike one love
and remember as payment
you'll owe me everything that you are

Simply strike one love
I even offer my favorite
there, she means nothing to me now

Simply strike one love
from my parade of fascinations
desires both quenched and undrunk

Simply strike one love
now give me an hour
to plot your descent into hell

Sitting on the curb in a parking lot behind the La Quinta

There is a moment of time when dusk and dawn
are indistinguishable
if you don't know your direction
and sitting on the curb in a parking lot
behind the La Quinta
my sense of time is shattered
periods of consciousness and utter nonexistence
are jagged pieces
a mosaic of the glass pieces of my sanity
I raise my head
and my neck still stiff from the seizure
and I imagine that it's getting lighter
but the air around me has a thickness that is new
and I can feel each kidney
buried in my back and aching
and I don't know how to move into the day
or the night
or the nothing
nothing at all
and I don't remember if I've smoked a cigarette
or if I'm smelling the butts
that have collected at this sitting spot
and if it gets lighter, I'll be able to walk
and return to my room
but I don't know if this is a dawn shard

or a dusk shard
and I think this was seizure number three
and I think I did smoke a cigarette
and I think maybe it will get lighter
and I don't want it to be night
and I'm sitting on the curb in a parking lot
behind the La Quinta
and I don't know what moment this is

I fell in love the other day

I fell in love the other day
again
for the umpteenth time

I was swept up and stolen away
and carried along on a jetstream of romance
and my heart was so completely filled

Because I fell in love the other day
again
and this time, she even spoke to me

I fell in love the other day
again
in a strip mall bookstore that smells of cat pee

I felt it coming with my first glance
and spent an hour trying to decide whether to
commit
and when I did, I let it hit me hard in the chest

Because I fell in love the other day
again
and I was unsure of her name

I fell in love the other day
again

a hard part in her hair and my soul

I found myself floundering to find myself
and decide who I would be if I became someone
who was in love with the woman across the room

I think of Lake Michigan with a storm far off
where the horizon bends
the winds and rain too far away to feel on my skin
churn the water
creating waves that rise and surge toward me
cresting in white foam
crashing into nothing as they near my feet
each wave a love as violent
as the storm that forces it on me
and the vanishes in a wash of bubbles

Because I fell in love the other day
again
soaking my socks and shoes

70 times 7

70 times 7 sins to atone
and still, many steps to go
calendar days blacked out with a Sharpie
the edge of my explorable world

to fall in love with fire
never crosses the mind of a saint
clean laundry and returned calls
are the accoutrements of the sane

but to wrap oneself in lies
an electric blanket against the cold
filled with dust mites and bed bugs
that only bite others

then the day came uninvited
over protestations and the gnashing of teeth
ripping my love from my arms
leaving me lonelier even than the moon

so, 70 times 7 sins to atone
and a request for a waiver for the rest
while I occasionally detect my old lovers' breath
her touch has almost faded

Sitting in a Starbucks

I'm sitting in a Starbucks in the middle of nowhere, Georgia, between court appearances, committed to writing a poem. But I have a terrible seat at a terrible table in a terrible location, and I can't see the first word from here. So, instead of writing I watch people but not for too long out of fear that they'll see me looking, and suddenly, I'll actually be here physically, in the room, and not a spectator, or a specter, a ghost.

I like people's faces when they don't know they are being seen when they don't even contemplate the possibility. They hardly ever smile, but they rarely frown. They hold their mouths steady, and only their eyes and brows move. Most people are pretty that way.

Occasionally, two or three, or four will cluster together and talk, emotions flashing across their faces, and then swap and switch among the group. A spiritual and communicative virus, but I don't like watching that as much. It makes me feel sad and alone like I want to be there, but my presence doesn't fit, so I look at others who are alone. Others who are looking for that first word.

The Sadness

I don't like it when the sadness comes
it fills the room around me like an odorless,
colorless gas
depriving my lungs of a tiny bit of the oxygen they
use
a felt/unfelt shroud

It's a pain without pain
like a knife in my chest, but I'm already numbed
a pressure and cutting, without the hurt
much like the anticipation of pain before a papercut
starts hurting

I don't like it when the sadness comes
and my soul feels exhausted, though my body isn't
and I wish a little that I was one of those who go to
bed for a week
but that limited crash is a luxury denied to me, so I
clean the house

It's a weakness without loss of strength
like I'm getting over a cold, but the sickness is gone
and the recovery is from the meds I took too often
each one without effect except to burn inside my
stomach

I don't like it when the sadness comes
both there and not, real and a figment
an imaginary friend that no one else believes in
but takes a chair in the corner of every room I enter
and I don't know its name

but it knows mine
and why mention it to others
they don't know what to say
takes thought
eats thought
gives a thought

and its very presence is so damn much work
like when I cleaned the fry vats at McDonalds when
I was in high school
and it smells the same even though it's odorless
but I said that already; it makes me repeat my
thoughts

I don't like it when the sadness comes
though I know it'll go away
we get tired of each other's company
and then I'll notice that it had left

so, I don't like it when the sadness comes
so I'll squint my eyes against the sun
so I'll spare others from my company
and so I'll pretend it isn't there

Virtue

"When does poetry become prose?"
she asked me
"When it's no longer true," I thought
but I lied and said, "I don't know."
"Formatting, I suppose."
after all, the young know nothing of virtue

They worship at the feet of purpose
and utility without vice
no passion to divert the course
three goals and a single objective
though that's just formatting, I suppose
after all, I am lucky to even be here

When I was a child, I dreamed of heroes
dragons, rings, and wars
and later, we seized buildings and sang songs
throughout the halls
but I see nothing of this wildness
though it's formatting, I suppose
after all, I'm no longer writing

One More Thing

"One more thing"
is how she'd signal
that our time together was done

always a throw-away
a request or a question
that never mattered

she was generous
but only to a point
and then the door closed

my heart would break
whenever she ended
and pulled away

but the thirst it created
for just another moment
would make me grasp

and hang on tightly
to what she smiling offered
her perpetual one more thing

Awe I Suppose

The Grand Canyon left me empty
a hollow gorge run through
too big to capture in a thought
best left to a postcard, I suppose

When I went to the Dali museum
in St. Petersburg, Florida, I stayed
at a hotel that had welcomed
Marlyn Monroe and Babe Ruth

The sprinkler pipes crisscrossed the ceiling
as tortuous as Dali's mustache
and I saw Picasso too and left
a cubist image of my face was my only takeaway, I
suppose

When my daughter was born
they split my wife open and
I dared to peek behind the curtain
she always says autopsy photos make us look like
chicken and smiles

I've been in rooms that I haven't
described to anyone, nor will I ever
some real, physical, and dark
some in my head, both lighter and darker, I suppose

I've never felt awe, not even once
though I've sought it out frequently
never seeing it as just up ahead
around the bend and behind the store

There are those who find it, or so they report
in music or nature or love
and though I doubt every claim that they make
still, I'm in awe of them, I suppose

Lame Horses

I despise short answers
with their brevity and focus
one, two, three-word replies
meant to carry us forward
lame horses and broken-winged birds

I am never "fine," or "swell,"
or "great," or "good."
my moods are a torrent of unpossessed feelings
and each a marching band of honking, plotting
geese
a thousand nonsensical thoughts and metaphors

I say I despise short answers, but I really hate you
able to sum up all of the surging stimuli
from within and without, and you expect me to nod,
and smile and pretend to understand

Thomas rages against the dark, and I want to join
him
but your silly, stupid words
stop everything so cold and sterile
that I lose my own soul to your impotence

So few words I hardly even wake up to you
like a brief reflection of a streetlight on a
windshield
driving past your room at night
I briefly open my eyes, but without purchase
I fade again

Your lack of loquaciousness, an asset
in the dirge-dance of daily life insults
not me, but the very nature of creation
which provides so many taunts and jabs
that you owe it a proper lament

To be one word or two, or three
in this muddy, drinking, sticky
and yes, glorious - truly glorious madness
impinging on our deepest hearts

I'm unsure if the greater hell is your single response
or my having to endure it
as if I'm the same, and if not
at least I'm complicit in the crime

"I despise short answers" is my only reply
when asked, "How's it going?" "What's up?" or
"Dinner?"
I'd rather turn up Brubeck
and wail than indulge in the play

But I'm also so tired and so unsure
of what an honest answer would sound like
that I know you'd rather not hear
I am tempted to reply with one, two, or three words
and leave the hornets inside me alone

still, I despise short answers
One, two, three
and I can't tell you what I really feel

11 A poem about a girl who is not named Grace

Grace is the breeze that carried her lightly
into my life and the wind, which
unexpectedly swept her away

I was tattered and shredded and too long between
drinks
when the room shifted enough
for our eyes to meet

and, given though I am to romance
and passion, I only saw sadness there
and I lost my footing

she took me home a building filled
with the dying, all the old and spent lives
except her place near the top

there were tubes and harsh chemicals and
embarrassed explanations
her lungs utterly broken
with a heart following suit

but her eyes were what had swallowed me
and had stolen away my breath, so I brushed them
aside
and slept that night in her bed

Grace is the breeze that carried her ashore
while I was still lost
and at sea

and I was more broken than even she was
though her eyes never brightened
or even shared a smile

when the wind swept her away
and I chose to move on
I was rarely too long between drinks

and I read that it was her breath that healed in due
time
while my own would continue
to struggle

still, I think of those eyes
when a breeze touches my neck
and I consider the fate of us both

It was a grace to me that carried her in and kept me
alive for a time
and a grace to her that carried her out
and granted a new life to her

Essay:
Writing, Dwelling, Art

(Writing)

I hate rhymes, I'm terrible at rhythm, and I have no sense of meter. This can be seen as a deficiency on my part or simply a preference. I'll concede the first but reject the second. My lack in this regard is acknowledged. But, it is not merely a preference. These things are alien to me. They are like a foreign language that is not translatable to my own. Why? Because I do not think in those ways. I have never stared out over a peaceful field where cows graze, and butterflies flit about and naturally rhymed "wide steer" with "my dear." When I consider what I am surveying, I do not think in iambic pentameter.

This is not a criticism of those for whom these devices are tools at hand. I respect those who wield them. In fact, I marvel at the ability. Reading these poets is like watching a great singer. I resonate with the lyrics and love the tune. I might even sing along in my car. But there is nothing in me that allows me to follow suit. I am not a singer. And if I try, it's poor karaoke at best.

The fact that I do not think or even experience the world in a rhyme/rhythm/meter way has an additional effect. If I attempt to write in this manner these tools distance me from my own experience. Poetry is an attempt to express my experience in this world. Therefore, my best poetry is the poetry that most directly expresses my experience. My goal is to produce a literary product that incarnates that experience. I approach poetry this way because I believe that artistic expression can be boiled down to a simple question: *"What color is the sky in your world?"*

(Dwelling)

So, why do I contend that all human expression can be boiled down to this question? Because human existence is fundamentally aloneness. In the language of the existentialists, we are thrown into the world, abandoned, and separated from others and creation itself. We are a thing apart. We are alone.

This aloneness extends beyond our first moments. The big-bang moment of aloneness, our birth, sends ripples out that confirm our separation. Even in our most intimate and connected times, there is a mismatch, a gap, an imperfect fit. Sometimes, it manifests itself as a failure to understand or a failure to communicate. Sometimes, it manifests as an outright conflict between individuals.

When I speak to another, I experience this separation because I hear their voice instead of my own. Regardless of how it manifests, on a fundamental level, whether we attempt to resolve it in relationships or cover it up with distractions, we are profoundly and irretrievably alone.

Every expressive act is a response to this aloneness. It is the individual calling out into the world. It is the echo of the individual's voice in the world seeking a response, waiting for an answer. Note it can also be more than this. There are many endeavors in this world where a person expresses their aloneness. Most politics, business, and, too often, religion is the expression of a person saying, "Listen to me," "Buy from me," or "Follow me." It is the person calling out and seeking an action from anyone who might hear.

(Art)

Art, though, is different. Art at its highest is not a demand for action or obedience from others. Art, in its best form, possesses a duality. The artist says, "This is my experience - what I see, hear, and feel. This is me. This is ME in my nakedness." But, it is not mere exhibitionism. It is not merely a body on a stage.

With art, the artist expresses themselves in their nakedness with a purpose different from that of the politician or capitalist. The artist expresses so that the other can find a connection by offering up a part of themselves in response. The artist does not say, "You! Do this!" The artist says, "This is me; come join me here." Art is a type of seduction wherein the artist presents themselves as both the place for connection and the manner of connection.

So, when I say that the artist is calling out, *"What color is the sky in your world?"* I am suggesting that artists offer their intimate experience of the world as a seduction to the other to engage and provoke their own experience of the world. This is done with the idea that the two, the artist and the other, can converge and join together in a deep congress.

So, rhyme, rhythm, and meter can be seen as a formalized system of courting. They are the stylized and codified techniques of intimacy. There are true masters of these forms. These grand romantics can waltz and flamenco with studied precision and are glorious. Watching these grand romantic artists at work, it is just as easy to be captivated by their technique as it is to be captured by their heart. It's like watching a comedian so skilled that instead of laughing at the joke, you respect the structure and execution. But, there is a marked difference between the experience of a joke and laughing with it. There is a difference between respecting artistry and experiencing art.

I am no technician. I prefer to present my art in the rawest form I can muster. When I attempt to show you the color of my sky, my goal is to go as deeply into expressing how it is for me to experience the sky that I see. I want to express the "grunt" or impact of experiencing the sky. That is, I want to put on the page the most immediate "ugh," the emotional and, dare I say, spiritual experience of the moment of experiencing the sky.

I do this because I want to know if I am truly alone. I want to know if I am a complete outsider. A mutant, a freak. Or if maybe, just maybe, a small part of what I experience in this world - whether you, too, experience it. Because, then, we are both not alone. And I would prefer that.

loneliness is the chill wind
created by the revolution of the Earth
as it spins through the void
so I call out to you
an incantation of hope
and forever await your reply

Third Row

We missed one another
you and I
though I sat in the third row weekly
and watched your show
occasionally to participate

We missed our mark
you and I
though our paths moved so closely together
one would have thought
we'd been joined

but I got sick for a time
a feverish and drunken brawl
with myself, I'm told
that left me toothless and weak when I walked

We missed our rally
you and I
I struggled to be what I thought
we both wanted me to be
but never was

We missed our day
you and I
and it was you who went mad and vanished
into a bat cave
and I bought a suit and tie

When I get sick for a time, I wonder
if it's a really good nap that I need

or to just lie in someone's bed
while they make me soup or tea

We missed a thing
you and I
but I wonder if you ever saw it, too
or if you had dinner plans
with a better record collection

and if I was too sick
for you and I

Tattoos

The tattoos on her arms recall a happier day
when friends gathered and drank and laughed
a reminder of that day, every day
even when she doesn't look
black lines on dark skin

Her hair pulled back, and her eyes downturned
her only companion in a suit, court-appointed
a day unanticipated on that inky night in June
signing the deal distractedly
black lines on white paper

They warned us about our permanent record
sins, crimes, and offenses preserved
each of us blind to the medium
but each notation absorbed so deeply
black lines on clear conscious

Dreams in sneakers

Life seems like a shorter period of time
than 25 years
when you are 20
and never expected to survive

The gulf of understanding between you and
consequence
feels like a moat
between you and a future
but still a tiny speck in God's eye

Not that you believe, but maybe you really do
too young to have resolved discrepancies
there are so many doubts
but you wear the cross your mom gave you

Life seems like an impossible period of time
as you try to recall your promise
from when you were young
and walked home with a backpack of A's and B's

The future was a voracious bitch that ate and ate
and ate
all the dreams you had in sneakers
and all the girls you wondered about
before these jumpsuit days

Kisses (Three Different Ones)

Kiss #1

I want to kiss you like I imagine Sarte kisses
the taste of coffee and cigarettes on your breath
my hand cupping the sharp line of your shoulder
blade
and no essence in this world

Do you dream of another when you're with me?
like I suspect Simone de Beauvoir did
of a languid woman in an apartment
who writes cliches' and lies

I want to kiss you like I imagine Sarte kisses
in a black suit and thin tie
my little round glasses
and you laugh because I am wall-eyed

I want it to be dangerous
and threaten all that I am
I haven't burned down my tower
more than a decade, it's been

I want to kiss you like it doesn't matter
yet we do it just because
the world is so damned black and white
we forget that we have claws

It was Camus that killed the stranger
and never shed a tear
and I was just as lonely
your hand brushes back your hair

I want to kiss you like I imagine Sarte kisses
and fade from public view
romance is in the ashes
and I exist in you

I want to kiss you like I imagine Sarte kisses
and then I'll just go home

Kiss #2

"Do you want to kiss me?" she asks
and I count to ten in my head
before I respond
without making any outward sign of my response
because that is a young man's idea of cool
movie star cool
but I'm not a movie star
and I'm neither a young man nor cool
but none of that matters
because this isn't really happening
I'm just imagining what if it did
how I'll respond if
"Do you want to kiss me?" she asks

Kiss #3

I don't remember our last kiss
but I do remember my first
cool summer night and the sky had faded
into dark blue and eventual black
we both sat waiting
as our friends receded to their homes

Things too often begin
immediately before an ending
and I was soon to leave

It was a sweet kiss
little more than a peck
and we both quickly rushed on home
I dare not count how long ago
we sat there waiting
as our youth receded to the stars

Things too often begin
immediately before an ending
and I was soon to leave

I don't remember our last kiss
the world was as brittle as rice paper then
even skin thins over time
and we moved from dark blue to black
we sat waiting together
while first kisses still held sway

Things too often begin
immediately before an ending
and I was soon to leave

3 Kisses (Reprise)

I want to kiss you like I imagine Sartre kisses.
Do you want to kiss me?
I don't remember our last kiss.

and I am soon to leave

Leaves

I love the fall leaves that turn brown
the best of them as big as your hand
and so dry they crunch like fresh potato chips
underfoot
and shatter into thousands of tiny puzzle pieces

They gather into great piles
in yards, along curbs, and crowded under bushes
to be kicked and tossed as I pass by
less joyfully than when I was young but still
beautiful

Occasionally, when the conditions are just right
a light breeze stirs a pile, and some of the leaves
rise
swirling in a column against reason and the gravity
of the world
the gust animating like a breath of life

And then it is gone, and the leaves collapse lifeless
falling, dead, and discolored at my feet
like my teeth, from my jaw
and I sigh at the long, hot summer end

It's been a year of hospitals; its defining trait
after Aspen, my cough wouldn't end
and my chest ground like it was filled
with crisp dead leaves

By the time I was released, I, again, had scars on
my lungs

but I'd entered due to a storm of chemistry
and my body, which once bleached my skin, turned me up
until I ran too hot to keep going

Outside my room, the leaves were not yet crisp
and the word "cancer" had come but went
while a drip drip drip slowed my body
and I secretly enjoyed the rest

When the leaves did turn and finally fell, so did my father
his stay was longer than mine, and he never left
it seemed his mind had slipped into a crack
and he saw all the tiny puzzle pieces and smiled

Hotels followed with Cane's chicken, coffee, and more travel
I took the lead where I could when needed
and walked every morning and night
the world crunching under my steps

Winter and spring came and went, and more travel
I don't recall much of those months
It's gotten so damned hot
and the ground so damned quiet
It was my sister's turn this time; guts twisted
I always write eulogies when people enter
it helps to bide your time while waiting
she is the only one of us left

I love the leaves that turn brown
the best of them as big as your hand

and so dry they crunch like fresh potato chips
underfoot
And shatter into thousands of tiny puzzle pieces

Isabella paints flowers

I don't have any make-up on
she objects and turns away
and her sweatshirt has more paint
than even the wall she faces

Billy Joel sings as if to her alone
in thanks, her hair matches the flowers
that she is conjuring to bless the wall
and I agree, Vienna waits for you

Isabella paints sunflowers while
Lindsey plays mandolin in my head, the room
her leaves remain only green smears
and she paints, never knowing what it means to me

we both wish there was no need to finish
but paint sets and drys without us
she fears completion, faces threatening failure
while I fear she'll stop tending blooms

Every Poem

an informal introduction to *vers chaotique*

every poem I write is a love song
every poem I write is a lament
every poem I write is a confession
      an admission
      a sin
      a deviation
      a violation
      a loss
      plea
      anguished cry
      outcry of loneliness
      cursing of others
            of myself
            of fate
            life
            pain
            pain and joy
            pain and joy and hope
            the hope that only exists in loss
and the hope that only exists in the anger and
confusion that is this fucking exhausting road race
and I want it to end
but not death
just my dinner and a discussion of the color of the
sky
and the color of the sky
and the color of your eyes
and mine
and to laugh

and fall
dangerously in love
with each other
and maybe
just maybe
ourselves

Cracks

I slip between the cracks, sometimes
and the whole room becomes a movie
people engaged in dialog
hitting their marks
playing to the crowd

meanwhile, I'm windswept,
and alone
between the cracks in my own soul

I grip the wheel firmer, in need
eavesdrop and study
notepad in hand
scribbling thoughts
they are all 3-D but muted

meanwhile, I'm windswept,
and alone
between the cracks in my own soul

I hold some memories too closely
reading the tea leaves in their cups
people make too many oaths
finding satisfaction in the words
moving easily about

meanwhile, I'm windswept,
and alone
between the cracks in my own soul

A second poem about a girl who isn't named Grace

She spoke to me one time
in her native accent
while we made love

An Australian girl with deeply sad eyes
to whom I owe a debt I'll never pay
And I probably love her, but I'll never know

But when she looked at me, she thought
this kid cuts

Around her throat, a silver pendant
a cross shape pressed in a square
and the chain I snapped one night and stole

I might have stolen her heart
I might have broken my word
I might have lost her name

But when she looked at me, she understood
this kid cuts

Kill Bill was a romance about a husband
leaving his wife for no better reason
than the fact that she loved him
too much, and she overflowed
and he could not share

he could not share

and she stopped his heart

I gave the cross back
a bit of personal redemption and
left in a U-haul alone

and when she reached out
married and well, I did not answer her call
though I should have

and when I look at myself
I know this kid cuts

Poem as Portraiture

Please take a seat
and cross your legs
smoke 'em if you got 'em
a long, slow drag on a cigarette
is the most intimate of gestures

Designer shoes
sleek Italian leather
black with pointy toes
shined to nearly a mirror
soles scuffed slightly to provide better traction

A glimpse of ankle
skin bare, clean, radiant
crisp dark slacks
a crease more accent than function
perfectly straight from knee to waist

I would paint you if I had that art
but I'm limited in my pallet
still, you brush my words away

A belt a half-inch wider
than I would have selected for you
but it highlights that you're long-waisted
in the manner of models today
and it suits whatever statement you are making

A shirt too white and open-collared
sleeves pushed up a bit
a surprising lack of jewelry

neither watch, nor ring, nor pin
anonymous in style and defiant in taste

Your hair is closely cut
eyes brighten when you smile
and you ask in a voice
a touch deeper than expected
"Where do we begin?"

I would compose a song to capture you
but I'm tone-deaf on my best day
still, you hum softly while waiting

Words are always deflections
diversions and false hints of paths
lies, delusions, and opacity
a brick wall built entirely on sand
language always misses
while you sit there in the gaps
It'd be easy to state the most obvious
the question on your lips
but I don't want this to end you
I prefer it when you're unsaid

I would take a photo of you
but my phone is rather old
still, you sit there and wait for more

On the One Year Anniversary of My Father's Passing – 09/06/24

I need a new forest green hoodie
the kind with the zipper up the front
because I hate pullovers
and the one that I bought
after you died
to walk back and forth for coffee
and to meet with morticians
and ministers
and buy flowers
get lunches
has developed a hole
it's crazy how quickly things fray

I need a new forest green hoodie
because we can never go back in time
and people always go away
but I would like to walk across those roads
past the gas station
toward the target
and get a fresh coffee
and snacks for the room
and return in time for TV
because I can't go back to when you were here
I'd like to revisit when your leaving was still new
it's crazy how quickly things fray

I'd say poems are like dandelions in a field behind the grade school if I thought you'd stay the night

I have four books, she says
and I scratch thick words on my screen
it would be so much easier
if I were young and the cost wasn't so great
and I could just run away to London or Vegas or
Brazil

Where the songs are sung in accented English

I wanted to write a song, but the best I can do
is steal snippets of conversations
that I can't help but overhear
because I eavesdrop and steal
like I'm one of Zevon's desperados crouching here
and we're both still getting sober

and the Beatles sing in an American accent again

I'm going to go up there and wing it
says a younger man so much sharper than I
but at least I'm fast and fearless
because my greatest failures are already public
and what the hell am I going to do anyway
I just want to sleep in your eyes tonight

and the music sounds efficient, but I've never been
good at inflection

Venus Growing Old

He had quit looking into mirrors a long time ago
so long ago that he'd forgotten which era
he last remembered looking into one
in high school, at a clothing store at the mall
he'd combed his hair straight, part on the side
and imagined, while not handsome, there was some
basic appeal

From college, there are no memories
of his own face or smile
he'd exiled his own reflection
after noting something there
that repelled and caused him shame
but it'd been so long
he couldn't be sure of what he'd seen

Venus was born to be a widow
Venus was born to one day grow old
Venus would gaze out of her window
Venus would slink off into the cold

His skin betrayed him one day
the site of his ever-losing war
he attacked himself as foreign
and salted his most intimate home
and the mirror became even less common
rushed when actually needed
an occasional glimpse at best

He covered his mouth while speaking
like Japanese girls in movies do

the razing it swept all over him
and his courage weakened and bowed
when alone he forgot his image
his thought only an avatar of himself
preserved in amber and a dream

Venus was born to be a widow
Venus was born to one day grow old
Venus would gaze out of her window
Venus would slink off into the cold

He had quit looking into mirrors
so very long ago
and didn't look again
until Venus was growing old

Read That Again

Read that again
the anonymous person ended their post
read that again
rage rises from my intestines through my stomach
and chocks my heart

Read that again
a command, a demand, an imperative
read that again
whether a shriek or a calm, sure voice
it seeks to compel me

I came to social media, I say
for news and friends and humor
cute dogs doing cute things to cute applause
but that's just a lie I tell myself
I come to be seduced
I come to have my desires caressed
and my interests piqued
to have my views gently and deliberately adjusted
I come to be swayed and romanced and
to have my very nature molded and shaped
to be made into someone with the very
desires that YES, they too can be perfectly satiated

But read that again
A demand put on me by an ungrateful lover
read that again
no better than "take out the garbage"
or "do your shoes belong in the hall"

I will accept, and I do embrace
the way you lull me and thrill
make me long
make me suffer
make me want
I submit to be your putty
your perfect creature
your most perfect consumer
all lust, desire, and self-loathing
seeking fulfillment in you
fulfillment in us
fulfillment to reach

read that again?
a garish reminder
a fourth wall broken
a spouse too absent
a lover too broken

So, I refuse to read that again

Remember to hug your guns tonight

Honesty is a virtue no one can afford
unless they're well-armed
with money, acclaim, and affirmation
hypnotized by the brightness of a better day
but to steal from Leonard, I'd tell you
you don't really care about laughter, do you

hug your guns tonight
and sing of fallen cradles
and hang a medal of St. Therese
devoted to Christ the child
and pray with them for each little flower
denied another day in the light

Tomorrow, we'll harden our buildings
our courts, and all the repercussions
but never our hearts, no, not our hearts
for the precious gifts of Adoni
and whisper gratitude that we get to be the ones
that hold them in our hands

hug your guns tonight
the Beatles are never wrong
but if happiness comes from a warm gun
then load them up with love
the quality of mercy is unmeasured
and feel their warmth tomorrow

values are just choices abstracted
and loves choice was never that hard
I could never pick one child over another

but still, they are simply bets placed
and the cylinder spins on
so hug your guns tonight

hug them til dawn

20 Poems

She said I'd probably write 20 poems
before I saw her again
I laughed and considered the compliment
the weather was turning colder, but had not yet
turned

She is one of those that chooses her words
carefully curating her selection
each passage begins like a premature child
her notebook an incubator of intent

I write nothing, of course
I stumble on paths through the woods that I know
and trip over stanzas at a ridiculous pace
and I run for 20 poems

Another produces works like flowers
gathered together in funerary bouquets
I laugh at her perfect rhythms
and I check the clouds for rain

I write nothing, of course
I float in the waves
and let the tides batter me
and I float for twenty poems

Then, he attempts to lead us
strutting with both passion and sound
a slender grasp on the future
when the ice will come on down

His language is explosive
part music, storm, and war
each presentation a volcano
his notebook just a song

I write nothing, of course
I merely sit and scratch
the letters that present themselves
20 poems in the sand

sadness just sometimes feels like another shade of tiredness

Sadness is the maroon to the red of tiredness

sadness is the richer, deeper, more complex
version of tiredness that you wake up with
because you overslept
but you cannot shake
and honestly
you're not sure you want to
'cause it's not worth the effort
and there is so much in maroon to explore

sadness is the Lou Reed to the Marky Mark of
tiredness

sadness is the dark and dingy street danger
version of tiredness that makes you want to shower
because it feels itchy
but the itch is inside
and not on the surface
you're not sure if this feeling is an abstraction
'cause it feels ever-present
and the bass line exactly syncs with your own
heartbeat

sadness is the battle at the end of the day
the too-harsh word at the tip of your tongue
the roll of your eyes when a friend is sincere
it is a pool of warm water that you just
want to throw yourself into
and sink and sink and sink and sink

and sink
and sink
and sink
and drown

sadness is the resignation to the relief of tiredness

sadness is the bone saw to the butterknife
version of tiredness destroying your ability to eat
because it chews up every intention and plan
but it has a will all its own, and that is such a
blessing
you're out of the decision-making business
'cause making a choice is so far beyond your reach
and why bother anyway

sadness is the addict uncle that pulls up
in your driveway and asks when your mom
will be home, and you barely recognize him
but you'd rather he just left

sadness is the teal to the green of tiredness
a deeper and more complex shade

Creativity

"What does creativity look like to you?"
the therapist asked, crossing his legs and readying
his pen

I look at him in a state of hatred and terror
the question a knife that'll slit
open my guts
and I'll spill out

a child with a bag
a dog with a bone
the pain in my knee
a call on the phone

all the pain I caused you when you wept at night
all the lies I told myself, I'm ugly in my sight

cars and leaves and God's loving grace
my anger, addiction, and self-destructive ways
I hate you, I love you, please just let me be
Bob Newhart, stop my heart
when I visit the sea

you ripped me, you tore me, dear God, make it stop
I can't look upon creativity, it is the fire of suns

home is

home is forever a place that was
a place I remember
no wait, that I recall
a glimpse of a past place
a rear-view image of an object
that is much further than it appears

home is more of a semblance of the familiar
a face, not that of a past friend or lover
but a person who could be their sibling
or cousin, more likely
or maybe just a clerk at the Kroger
where mom used to shop

home is never an is
only a was
or perhaps a will be
or should be
or should have been
could have been

home is that ramshackle house
assembled of the driftwood of my memories
the smell of the wind off the lake
and the story you might have heard
that isn't quite true
but now exists as a memory

Knick-Knack

Knick-Knack Jack Kerouac
I feel so sad to read you
slow blues guitar makes me ponder
why I never really knew you

Anthony was a Cali boy
filled with love and heroin
while I was more traditional
and drank through all my sin

music leads me walking
a shame that I could never sing
but your stream of conscious nonsense
keeps me honest occasionally

I hate the fucking talking
will you shatter my resolve
and fill me with antagonism
that drags me underground

Jack Kerouac, please save me
and deliver me from evil
dharma drums and heartbeat thuds
it's all one roll of paper

but the rhythm it returns to me
in spite of all the glamour
I don't understand near as well
as I love your black and white photo

I wish I could write emotions
as rich as a guitar note
but the pain that music causes me
can't be captured in a stroke

Knick-Knack Jack Kerouac
Knick-Knack and a chat with Sha
Ryan, please play for me
as I drift into the wall

Knick-Knack Jack Kerouac
Can I call you Jean-Louis?
Knick-Knack Jack Kerouac
I'm forever in your debt

Sad Faces

Sad faces are preferable to happy ones
wide, hollow eyes draw me in
a silken web
and my longing finds a home

happy faces shut me out
white teeth and glinting eyes
a movie premiere spotlight
I shrink and mentally go fetal

sad faces set the table
jaws held still and noncommittal
drawn entirely of lines
you are a blanket for my cold

happy faces frighten me
they demand I comply in joy
a whirlwind in my ears
I leave all your parties early

sad faces are preferable to happy ones
each blemish and scar is a beauty
the void-space of starlessness
we orbit the same moon

Retirement

The letter says I can start collecting my pension
now
which feels like a cruel joke
that it is the opening line to the last chapter of a
book
or a part thereof

The letter promises a miserably small amount of
money
and I can still work
so what the hell does this really mean to collect
retirement
did I win or lose

The letter says that a delay will not increase my
benefits
which feels like a warning
I've already delayed becoming what I want to be
but it says I can still work at it

little frustrations

little frustrations spiderweb the windshield of my
outer demeanor
while a war of attrition wages between my better
angel and my anger at the world
slug it out behind my eyes
and in my stomach
making me roll my eyes
and piss you off

little frustrations collect like dead skin cells on the
dash of my car
and join with bits and crumbs of rushed unhealthy
lunches
piling up higher
like a grey garden
and if I brush them away
they swirl in the air around me

I've never been the better man
I've never been that bad
I've never understood the calm
demanded of the hero

little frustrations are the drunken birds that fly into
my windows
after eating wild grapes that fermented on the vine
because the weather was just right
and my frustration turns to exasperation
and turns upon others
turns upon myself
turns everyone away

I've never been a peaceful man
I've never been that evil
I've never really felt the calm
that settles in the middle

little frustrations spiderweb the windshield of my
outer demeanor
and obscure my vision of the road ahead

Surrender

"What does it feel like to surrender?" she asks as
she scratches an old stick match to life on the sole
of her shoe and lights a cigarette she seemingly
produced from thin air, and then pulls a long drag

"Feel?," I reply
it smells like burnt plastic
through your car's air vents
on a ride home
alone
in the dark
          you forgot your wallet
and fuck that guy anyway!
the gas gauge is low
your range is 37 miles
          home is 38
the road keeps rising
fighting gravity
fighting the weight of the car
and you don't know how long you can do this
the mist is gathering on the windshield
but you won't turn on your wipers
until its almost
almost
too late

"What does it feel like to surrender?" she asks and
brushes a few strands of hair back and tucks them
behind her ear before she uses both hands to smooth
back her slick oily hair.

"Feel?" I reply
it tastes like too much salt
when you are cooking for a third date
and GrubHub takes 40 minutes
        and she'll be here in 35
you confused the salt and sugar
Chinese food is so hard
and shit you're no goddamn gourmet
soy sauce stains so easily
you really wanted to be cool
        classy
but your anger is rising
all you can feel is gravity
the weight of the failure
and you don't know how long you can do this
you're sweating from the heat
and the resignation
until it's almost
almost
too late

"What does it feel like to surrender?" she asks, and
for the first time in my life I realize that I've never
really thought about the question and she smiles
with a look in her eyes that tells me she knows that.

"Feel?" I reply
it sounds like that music
that begins as background
but creeps into you
and pushes away everything
that is just killing you and the moment
until it takes over

and Jesus on the shore!
I love this song
love that lyric right there
wish I could hit repeat
with each breath the volume is rising
nothing else defies the gravity
or the weight of this instant
and you don't know how long you can do this
but if you can just stay in this song
you nearly miss your cue
until it's almost
almost
too late

Crazy

To those who have gone crazy
and descended into their own depths
and explored the old mining shafts
of anguish, pain, betrayal, and regret
I hear you

To those who have gone crazy
condemned to it by their own hand
who committed the great sacrilege
of tempting fate with their own annihilation
I see you

bobbing to the surface
every 5 to 10 days
to see if the world is still there
and pay the rent
so poisoned that even
the sun and air sting
half as much
as your kidneys ache

To those who have gone crazy
in an act of defiance against their own self
and somehow found a back stairwell home
but never completely
I love you

if you don't mind

if you don't mind
I'd like to not like you for a while
it's almost certain
not to be permanent or even long-term
but right now, I don't
really like you

the world itself grows weary
of me at twice the rate
as I come to tire of you
and your presence in my space
and in my mind, I don't
really like you

day to day feelings
have nothing to do
with the tides that batter our lives
all salinity and spiteful
still, I know I'll love you once again
but today, I don't really like you

Wonder

I wonder where they all went
and if they'd slipped away in the dead of night
there were so many already where I thought I was
running
where too bold first steps were taken
and sincere promises were made
with no possibility of being fulfilled

I wonder if I ever met the great ones
men and women of tomorrow who would make the
world shine
spinning gold from peanut shells
and posing for family photographs
sublimely happy just being the right sort of people
with bright Crest smiles

I wonder, too, about the artists I knew
most condemned to fail in the end
or end up baking eclairs in storefronts filled with
fairy lights
I miss them the most of all
and the writers and the dreamers
who passed me by, though I pushed

I wonder why they all left me behind

Platonic Love Poems

There are no truly Platonic love poems
because that's not what love means
love is the incarnation of intimacy
it is the urge, command, demand
of the flesh to feel its own heat
reflected back upon itself
after warming the flesh of another

There is no truly Platonic love
because that's not what love is
love is the incarnation of communion
it is the reaching, grasping, searching out
of <u>this</u> hand, <u>this</u> heart, to yours
and drawing you closer to me
against the mirror tug of you pulling me

I love you, I love you, I love you
I call it out 330 million times
each one a separate name of God
a request to be held

There is no truly Platonic
because we are not mere forms
we are matter and spirit inseparable
and our hands, our hearts, our teeth
hunger for so much more
than the loneliness of the void

we are all so far apart

There are no truly Platonic love poems
because we must never be left alone
and although we never physically touch
we'll twist and entwine like lovers
we are spit and flesh and bone
and love that is itself a body
that is more than Academy stone

Poet

I decided to call myself a poet
because I had run out of all other rebellion
the world had cast me in a role
a minor character in a play
who believed himself to be the star

How I fought for that stardom
I fought the world and expectations
I fought every idea of who I was to be
and I poisoned myself and bled
just to make you all notice

But all my successes and all my feats
titles, labels, roles, and good seats
dragged me further and further
away from who I thought I could be

So, I decided to call myself a poet
and write poetry
because only a fool would choose this
getting off the wheel and on the road
with only chaotic verse as a map

Acknowledgments

I want to acknowledge and thank my wife, LaDonna, for supporting the insane idea, "At sixty, I think I'll become a poet," and for indulging this weird journey. You have enabled me to fulfill a dream. And to my daughter, Ella, you are the most creative artist I have ever known. Thank you for inspiring me to work on my own art.

To Deanna Repose Oaks, thank you for challenging me to write poetry and for nudging me on stage. I love reading my poetry before a crowd more than anything. To Yong Takahashi, you are an inspiration, asking the question, "Why not do every kind of art?"

Thank you to Sean Mills; you gave me space to speak. SR Butler, for being my first teacher of poetry. To Huang Sha, who reminded me of the beauty in my words, and Uddipana Goswami, for writing words that make me reach for more. To Cleopatra Sorina Illescu and Sue Aughi, who remind me of the music behind it all. And finally, my mother, who would have loved to see this book in print, and my father, who never would have doubted I could do it.

Thank you all. I hope you like what I've put together.

About the Author

Kevin Schumaker was educated to be a philosophy professor, became a lawyer, and made a number of good choices and a lot more bad ones. Throughout it all, he has loved words more than anything else. Whether it be the novels of Camus and Vonnegut, the philosophy of Sartre and Foucault, the comedy of Carlin and Martin, or the lyrics of Bowie and Rundgren - words and the way they tumble forward ignoring all rules to connect one with another, one person with another. Words have always been his companion and best friend.

Born in Wisconsin in a new subdivision in the middle of nowhere and far from the city center, Kevin has tried to craft a world from the existential heart of American hopes, dreams, addictions, loves, danger, and lies. This is his first attempt to put his vision on paper.

peace be with you